# Simple Secrets

## GOLDEN NUGGETS FROM GOD'S WORD TO ENHANCE YOUR MARRIAGE

WESLEY & NEESHA STRINGFELLOW

SIMPLE SECRETS
*Golden Nuggets from God's Word to Enhance Your Marriage*

Wesley & Neesha Stringfellow
Post Office Box 116
Flossmoor, Illinois 60422

Heartlifetoday.org

HearLife Ministries
Post Office Box 116
Flossmoor, Illinois 60422

Copyright © 2017 Wesley & Neesha Stringfellow
ISBN #978-1-943343-75-1

Destined To Publish
www.destinedtopublish.com

# DEDICATION

This book is dedicated to every married couple who thought they couldn't make it, to every couple who wondered why your marriage isn't the fairy tale you signed up for, and to every couple who has purposed in your hearts to have a healthy marriage, this book is for you.

Whether you are newlyweds or have been married over 50 years, God intended for us to enjoy the abundance of life, and that definitely includes marriage.

Every married couple will have a trial or two in their life, but if you practice our simple secrets, you can have a joyful and prosperous marriage.

# Simple Secrets

# Introduction

Dear Couples,

The beauty of marriage we know comes from the creator God Almighty.

*God is the one who patterns the body of Christ to marriage.*

Marriage isn't just an arrangement; it's an intimate and personal way for us to share the love of God with the world. But the great expectation of having a fairy tale marriage has a tendency to scare many couples.

God did not intend for marriage to be a scary trial in your life. He placed in the hearts of every human the desire not to be alone. His intention was for two to become one and a covenant union to be birthed, experiencing the joys of life together.

Although every couple's story starts out differently, many couples enter into their marriage covenant the wrong way, having preconceived notions. We believe there are golden nuggets you can practice along with God's Word that can bring a special touch of unity to your marriage.

In this book, we share a few Simple Secrets to having a fun-filled, healthy marriage. Over the last 29 years, we have learned that it's the *simple* things in a marriage that make a difference. These practices have become a staple in our relationship. They keep us connected.

Use this book as a tool to help you create strategies for your marriage that will help you enjoy one another.

Because what you learn will last a lifetime, you can share these simple secrets with your children and grandchildren, leaving a legacy of beautiful marriages – it does not have to be scary or hard work.

---

*Proverbs 27:17 (KJV)*

*"Iron sharpeneth iron; so a man sharpeneth the countenance of his friend."*

---

In a nutshell, its so important to us that couples make it, it's vital to the next generation, and not just make it but to really embrace and enjoy the journey called marriage.

So, no matter what stage of marriage you are in, try these simple secrets, and you will welcome a long-lasting marriage and friendship for a lifetime.

Remember, you are never to young or old to start practicing the simple secrets to keep your marriage healthy. Everyone has something to offer, be encouraged to start.

# NEVER TOO YOUNG OR OLD

Couples get married for numerous reasons, we hope the main reason was love. But why is it that so many couples choose divorce? We believe there are some simple secrets and principles that couples should practice in order to live out an enjoyable life with one another.

We believe secrets are hidden from our everyday practical lifestyles. Why is it a secret you might ask? Simply because we missed it. We make things harder than they truly have to be.

One of the main complaints from couples is the lack of communication, or not having effective communication, and yes this may be true, but what if we began to practice the simple things in life that will enhance our marriage? What would happen if we took those simple nuggets and apply them? Guess what? You will also have an opportunity to make a simple secret list of your own.

We pray this will bring another perspective to enjoying your married life, perhaps you practice these simple secrets already, then we encourage you to make a list of your own and share them. You are never too young or old to learn or adapt new and old tools to help strengthen your marriage.

God Bless You

Wes & Neesha

There are no secrets between husbands and wives

Before you even continue reading another page, make a declaration that you don't and won't keep any secrets. The secret to love is in truth and sharing your entire life with your spouse.

MR. _____

MRS. _____

# INTRODUCTION

---

*Matthew 6:21*
*For where your treasure is,*
*there will your heart be also.*

# Not-So-Simple Secrets

It's important to share everything. Couples who keep secrets, slowly seek to separate. Like a slow leaky faucet, overtime it can do major damage. Your spouse should be your best friend and the only secret should be, simply no secrets.

The only secret should be the excitement you share with each other about what God has in store for you in your Marriage and anticipate the great things He is going to do through the both of you.

---

*I Corinthian 2:9-10 LEB*

*But just as it is written, "Things which eye has not seen and ear has not heard, and which have not entered the heart of man, all that God has prepared for those who love him" For to us God revealed them through the spirit; for the spirit searches all things, even the depths of God.*

---

# REFLECTIONS

List the goals you desire for your marriage.

.................................................................................................................................

.................................................................................................................................

Share with your spouse your hearts' desires by writing them down.

.................................................................................................................................

.................................................................................................................................

Pray a simple prayer together daily, with anticipation.

.................................................................................................................................

.................................................................................................................................

Write down a scripture that will bring life to your unity.

.................................................................................................................................

.................................................................................................................................

.................................................................................................................................

.................................................................................................................................

# PRAYER & WORSHIP

Give each day Prayer Praise and Worship. Practice doing a devotional together daily, even if it's only one verse and a small prayer. This recipe will change your life.

Couples have busy lives, and it may not be that simple to follow every day, however make it a point to at least try.

Couples that pray together stay together.

---

*Psalm 16:11 NRSV*

*You show me the path of life. In your presence there is fullness of joy; in your right hand are pleasures forevermore.*

---

# REFLECTIONS

How often do you Pray with your spouse?

.......................................................................................................................

.......................................................................................................................

Write down a scripture that will bring life to your praise and worship.

.......................................................................................................................

.......................................................................................................................

Find a couple's devotional you would like to study together.

.......................................................................................................................

.......................................................................................................................

Write down how often you realistically can spend some time praying and worshipping with your spouse.

.......................................................................................................................

.......................................................................................................................

.......................................................................................................................

# HUGS & KISSES!

Hug & Kiss your spouse every morning and night Greet your spouse with a kiss, leave your spouse with a kiss, an intentional kiss, It will become habitual.

Make it a point to hug each other and don't rush, take your time, it simply keeps you connected.

---

*Colossians 3:14 (ESV)*

*"And above all these put on love, which binds everything together in perfect harmony."*

---

# REFLECTIONS

How often do you desire to hug and kiss?

..................................................................................................................

..................................................................................................................

Is it important to practice some form of physical connection daily?

..................................................................................................................

..................................................................................................................

Write down what form of physical connection is your desire.

..................................................................................................................

..................................................................................................................

Write down a scripture that will bring life to your connection.

..................................................................................................................

..................................................................................................................

..................................................................................................................

# PRIORITY

Make your spouse your #1 priority.

Your spouse should be number one, over everyone. They should come first – yes, over parents, children, job, church. If you are number one in each other's lives, everything else will simply be just fine. We as couples have a tendency to put everything and everyone else first, but our connection should be stronger than every connection in the human world.

If we are number one in each other's lives, everything else will be accomplished with ease.

---

*John 15:12-14 (NLT)*

*"This is my commandment: Love each other in the same way I have loved you. There is no greater love than to lay down one's life for one's friends. You are my friends if you do what I command."*

---

# REFLECTIONS

How do you make your spouse a priority?

.................................................................................................

.................................................................................................

.................................................................................................

.................................................................................................

What areas can SIMPLY show them that they are your priority?

.................................................................................................

.................................................................................................

.................................................................................................

.................................................................................................

Write down a scripture that will bring life to your priorities.

.................................................................................................

.................................................................................................

.................................................................................................

# R.E.S.P.E.C.T.

♥ **Respect** your spouse for their strengths and never look down on them for their weaknesses.

♥ **Exhort** your spouse daily. Everybody has flaws, and it's easy for us to point them out, and sometimes hold grudges. But if you as a couple respect your strengths in each other, it will build you and your spouse up and not tear you down.

♥ **Support** each other in your dreams and endeavors.

♥ **Pray** for one another always.

♥ **Celebrate** each other, and all the good things that you see.

♥ **Trust** the God in each other. By trusting the God in each other, you both should set out to respect your walk with God, and then you will continue to value and respect each other always.

---

*Romans 12:10 (ESV)*

*"Love one another with brotherly affection. Outdo one another in showing honor."*

---

# REFLECTIONS

Create your own SIMPLE acronym for RESPECT in your marriage.

........................................................................................................................................

........................................................................................................................................

........................................................................................................................................

........................................................................................................................................

........................................................................................................................................

Write down a scripture that will bring respect and honor to your marriage.

........................................................................................................................................

........................................................................................................................................

........................................................................................................................................

........................................................................................................................................

........................................................................................................................................

........................................................................................................................................

# DECISIONS

ALWAYS include your spouse in every decision!

Don't exclude your spouse from anything; their opinion is important and they matter, even if they never act like they care or want to be included.

---

*Ephesians 5:33 (NLT)*

*So again I say, each man must love his wife as he loves himself, and the wife must respect her husband.*

---

# REFLECTIONS

Reflect on decisions where you may not have included your spouse.

........................................................................................................................

........................................................................................................................

........................................................................................................................

Make a declaration to SIMPLY include your spouse in every decision.

........................................................................................................................

........................................................................................................................

........................................................................................................................

Write down a scripture that will bring life to making great decisions.

........................................................................................................................

........................................................................................................................

........................................................................................................................

........................................................................................................................

# HAPPY START = HAPPY END

How you start the day makes all the difference!

Start the day with a compliment or a word of affirmation. Leave love notes on the pillow or next to the toothbrush. This simple affirmation will fill up your love tank.

*1 Thessalonians 3:12 (NLT)*

*"And may the Lord make your love for one another and for all people grow and overflow…"*

# REFLECTIONS

How can you simply commit to start your day?

.................................................................................................................

.................................................................................................................

What does that look like for your home?

.................................................................................................................

.................................................................................................................

In what area can you fill up your and your spouse's love tanks?

.................................................................................................................

.................................................................................................................

Write down a scripture that will fill up love in your life.

.................................................................................................................

.................................................................................................................

.................................................................................................................

.................................................................................................................

# Music Is Key

What's your favorite song? What's your spouse's favorite song? It's important to have a song, and to enjoy filling your home with music.

Music makes everything better – it stimulates the brain and other parts of your body. Play music that brings back great memories and puts you in the mood for love.

Choose your favorite song or playlist, and simply make music together.

*Psalm 101:1 (NLT)*

*"I will sing of your love and justice, Lord. I will praise you with songs."*

# REFLECTIONS

Make a list of ten or more of your favorite songs – it simply will send sparks!

........................................................................................

........................................................................................

........................................................................................

........................................................................................

........................................................................................

........................................................................................

Write down a scripture that speaks to music in your life.

........................................................................................

........................................................................................

........................................................................................

........................................................................................

........................................................................................

........................................................................................

# THINK BEFORE YOU SPEAK

Check your response before opening your mouth – words are hard to take back.

Our mouths can get us in trouble, so let's check ourselves and our motives before we respond. This is a simple vital nutrient for every marriage.

---

*Ephesians 4:29 (ESV)*

*"Let no corrupting talk come out of your mouths, but only such as is good for building up, as fits the occasion, that it may give grace to those who hear."*

---

# REFLECTIONS

Reflect on a time when you could have SIMPLY thought before you spoke.

........................................................................................................................

........................................................................................................................

........................................................................................................................

In what ways can you improve in this area?

........................................................................................................................

........................................................................................................................

........................................................................................................................

Write down a scripture that talks about the power of the tongue and our speech.

........................................................................................................................

........................................................................................................................

........................................................................................................................

........................................................................................................................

# SWEET SLEEP

Never go to bed angry. Make it a point to always end the evening with peace, even if there is only a small point of contact.

You might have a disagreement, but always connect before you go to sleep – it's a simple antidote for recovery and making up.

*Ephesians 4:26 (MSG)*

*"Go ahead and be angry. You do well to be angry – but don't use your anger as fuel for revenge. And don't stay angry. Don't go to bed angry. Don't give the Devil that kind of foothold in your life."*

# REFLECTIONS

How often do you go to bed angry? How can you choose to make peace before sleep?

........................................................................................................................................

........................................................................................................................................

........................................................................................................................................

Come up with a SIMPLE strategy together and write down your point of truce so you can use it to never go to bed angry.

........................................................................................................................................

........................................................................................................................................

........................................................................................................................................

Write down a scripture that speaks to sweet sleep.

........................................................................................................................................

........................................................................................................................................

........................................................................................................................................

........................................................................................................................................

# FILL UP THE LOVE TANK

Practice actions that your spouse loves, not just what you love. Every couple's tank can run low at times, but do you know what fills up your spouse's love tank?

Ask your spouse often what they like . . . what they love. Then find ways to surprise them; it's a simple, powerful addition to your marriage.

*Psalm 103:5 (NLT)*

*"He fills my life with good things. My youth is renewed like the eagle's!"*

# REFLECTIONS

Are you guilty of starving your spouse from what they need?

Hey honey, so here it is ......

......................................................................................................................

......................................................................................................................

......................................................................................................................

What SIMPLE gift of love can you give your spouse to fill up their love tank?

......................................................................................................................

......................................................................................................................

......................................................................................................................

Write down a scripture that speaks to loving your spouse.

......................................................................................................................

......................................................................................................................

......................................................................................................................

# DON'T BE RUDE, DUDE

Avoid speaking rudely or abruptly to your spouse, especially in public. Every couple has a disagreement at times, but one thing you should never do is disrespect each other.

Make it a point to never name-call, and find a way to handle your conflict without tearing each other down. Intense fellowship is good, but not if it leaves the other spouse dejected.

*Ephesians 4:29 (NCV)*

*"When you talk, do not say harmful things, but say what people need – words that will help others become stronger."*

SIMPLY avoid rudeness.

........................................................................................................................

........................................................................................................................

What tactics can you use to avoid being rude or inconsiderate toward your spouse?

........................................................................................................................

........................................................................................................................

Write down ways you can SIMPLY build up your spouse and not tear them down.

........................................................................................................................

........................................................................................................................

Write down a scripture that speaks of your words.

........................................................................................................................

........................................................................................................................

........................................................................................................................

# SPICE IT UP!

Never take each other for granted. If the flavor in your marriage is dull and has no taste, add some spice. Couples that fall into the mediocrity of marriage can find themselves in a trap of no return.

Be intentional about being engaged, making sure you are not just going through the motions. Pray for wisdom to keep things exciting in your marriage.

*Jeremiah 33:3 (NASB)*

*"Call to Me and I will answer you, and I will tell you great and mighty things, which you do not know."*

# INTRODUCTION

Does your marriage still have flavor?

..................................................................................................................................................

..................................................................................................................................................

What SIMPLE areas need to be spiced up?

..................................................................................................................................................

..................................................................................................................................................

Share with your spouse a SIMPLE list of where you desire to add more flavor.

..................................................................................................................................................

..................................................................................................................................................

Write down a scripture from Song of Solomon that will add poetry to your love.

..................................................................................................................................................

..................................................................................................................................................

..................................................................................................................................................

# SEEK WISE COUNSELING

Every counselor needs a counselor, and it's always important to improve your relationship.

Never be ashamed to reach out for help. Oftentimes, couples should choose individual counseling – going together is great, but it is good to seek wise counsel for yourself as well.

*Proverbs 11:14 (KJV)*

*"Where no counsel is, the people fall: but in the multitude of counsellors there is safety."*

# REFLECTIONS

Why is it so difficult for couples to SIMPLY seek counsel?

.............................................................................................................

.............................................................................................................

Do you personally believe seeking counsel is necessary?

.............................................................................................................

.............................................................................................................

Set a goal where you will commit to seeking wise counsel.

.............................................................................................................

.............................................................................................................

Write down a scripture that speaks to wise counsel.

.............................................................................................................

.............................................................................................................

.............................................................................................................

.............................................................................................................

# TALK ABOUT IT

BE HONEST! Tough talks are necessary. Talk about the difficult things, no matter how hard it is.

Make sure you understand what your spouse is saying and where they are coming from.

Shutting down will only lead to experiences that will be more painful than having tough talks from the beginning.

*Proverbs 24:26 (NRSV)*

*"One who gives an honest answer
gives a kiss on the lips."*

# REFLECTIONS

What conversations are SIMPLY difficult to have with your spouse?

.................................................................................................................

.................................................................................................................

Write down topics that are difficult to share with your spouse.

.................................................................................................................

.................................................................................................................

List the SIMPLE ways you can avoid shutting down or shutting out your spouse.

.................................................................................................................

.................................................................................................................

Write down a scripture that speaks to communication.

.................................................................................................................

.................................................................................................................

.................................................................................................................

# TRUE FRIENDS

Check on your honey bun. Do weekly check-ins on your spouse and make sure they are okay. Friends love to talk to each other and share their heart.

Never assume that all is well and everything is good, because it may not be. Check-ins keep you both on the same page.

---

*Proverbs 18:24 (NRSV)*

*"Some friends play at friendship, but a true friend sticks closer than one's nearest kin."*

---

*Ephesians 4:2 (NLT)*

*"Always be humble and gentle. Be patient with each other, making allowance for each other's faults because of your love."*

---

# REFLECTIONS

How often would you like to check in with your spouse?

.................................................................................................................................

.................................................................................................................................

.................................................................................................................................

In what SIMPLE areas do you build your friendship with your spouse?

.................................................................................................................................

.................................................................................................................................

.................................................................................................................................

Write down a scripture that speaks to friendship.

.................................................................................................................................

.................................................................................................................................

.................................................................................................................................

.................................................................................................................................

.................................................................................................................................

# I SEE YOU

New clothes? New haircut? Weight loss? Promotion?

Are you paying attention to what's going on in the life of your spouse? Something as small as a husband changing his haircut or a wife getting her eyebrows arched can be missed.

Always keep your eyes open for changes. It's so important to affirm and compliment your spouse. Acknowledge and find the best in them, talk about it, and celebrate them.

---

*2 Corinthians 9:8 (ISV)*

*....God is able to make every blessing of yours overflow for you, so that in every situation you will always have all you need for any good work.*

---

# REFLECTIONS

Have you seen any SIMPLE changes in your spouse?

.................................................................................................................................

.................................................................................................................................

How often do you see your spouse?

.................................................................................................................................

.................................................................................................................................

Write a list of amazing attributes for your spouse, letting them know you see them.

.................................................................................................................................

.................................................................................................................................

Write down a scripture that can encourage

.................................................................................................................................

.................................................................................................................................

.................................................................................................................................

.................................................................................................................................

# ROMANCE ON THE RANGE

Love is in the food, so cook a meal together at least once a week.

Allow love to be in your food – making love (cooking, that is) in the kitchen can allow the fire to burn. While you cook together, it creates great harmony in communication.

Even if you are not the greatest cook, you can help prepare, stir, and clean. Embrace the idea that cooking in the kitchen can set a blaze in your loins for love.

---

*1 Corinthians 10:31 (BSB)*

*So whether you eat or drink or whatever you do, do all to the glory of God.*

---

# REFLECTIONS

How often do you cook a SIMPLE meal together?

..............................................................................................................

..............................................................................................................

Write down a day where you can create romance in the kitchen together once a week.

..............................................................................................................

..............................................................................................................

Write down SIMPLE meals that you enjoy together.

..............................................................................................................

..............................................................................................................

Write down a scripture that speaks to working together.

..............................................................................................................

..............................................................................................................

..............................................................................................................

..............................................................................................................

# MONEY MATTERS

Be a wise steward over your money: talk about your money, set goals, create a budget.

Be aware of what's going on in your finances. There is always a chief financial officer in the marriage, but they should never work alone.

Husbands and wives should both be knowledgeable about their money.

---

*Luke 12:15 (NLT)*

*"Beware! Guard against every kind of greed. Life is not measured by how much you own."*

---

# REFLECTIONS

Write down areas where you SIMPLY desire to see improvement with your money.

........................................................................................

........................................................................................

........................................................................................

Set SIMPLE Goals of unity by writing them down.

........................................................................................

........................................................................................

........................................................................................

Write down a scripture that speaks to what God says about money.

........................................................................................

........................................................................................

........................................................................................

........................................................................................

........................................................................................

# LAUGHTER IS A MEDICINE

Laugh together at least once a day. Laugh, laugh, and laugh some more — never stop.

There is healing in laughter. Find moments to enjoy one another, reminisce about old funny stories, and be silly together.

Enjoy one another.

*Proverbs 17:22 (NLT)*

*"A cheerful heart is good medicine, but a broken spirit saps a person's strength."*

# REFLECTIONS

How many times do you SIMPLY laugh?

..........................................................................................................................

..........................................................................................................................

..........................................................................................................................

Write down five SIMPLE things that make you laugh.

..........................................................................................................................

..........................................................................................................................

..........................................................................................................................

Write down a scripture that speaks to laughter.

..........................................................................................................................

..........................................................................................................................

..........................................................................................................................

..........................................................................................................................

..........................................................................................................................

# SHHHH... ARE YOU LISTENING?

Take the time to listen with your whole heart. Listening with your whole heart means you hear me even without words. Nothing should catch you off guard if you are listening. Every spouse should be aware when changes are taking place.

Listen out for what your spouse is really saying – be attentive to the heart of the matter. If you are listening, you will avoid many pitfalls and traps along the way of life.

Stop talking so much – quiet your spirit and listen to what is being said from the heart.

*Luke 6:45 (NASB)*

*"...for his mouth speaks from that which fills his heart."*

# REFLECTIONS

In what SIMPLE areas do you need to listen more?

.................................................................................................

.................................................................................................

.................................................................................................

Write a list of ten areas where you can listen more with your whole heart.

.................................................................................................

.................................................................................................

.................................................................................................

Write down a scripture that speaks to hearing.

.................................................................................................

.................................................................................................

.................................................................................................

.................................................................................................

.................................................................................................

# STAY HEALTHY

Caring for your health is caring for your spouse.

We often take our physical bodies for granted, and we don't care for ourselves the way we should. You might not have not practiced great healthy habits when you first got together as a couple, but it's never too late to start. Keep up the temple God has given you. Encourage one another not just by verbal action but by getting in the trenches with your spouse. It's for both of you. Always take the time to schedule physical fitness activities for strengthening your body and soul. At least once a week, do some type of physical activity.

Set goals and stick to them – eat healthy, exercise together. If you don't have energy physically, you won't have the stamina for much else.

*3 John 2 (KJV)*

*"Beloved, I wish above all things that thou mayest prosper and be in health, even as thy soul prospereth."*

Make a list of five SIMPLE SECRETS you can both do to stay healthy.

..................................................................................................................................

..................................................................................................................................

..................................................................................................................................

..................................................................................................................................

..................................................................................................................................

Write down a scripture that speaks to health.

..................................................................................................................................

..................................................................................................................................

..................................................................................................................................

..................................................................................................................................

..................................................................................................................................

# LOVE AMORE IN ACTION

Make love often. You are never too old for some love making. And have sex too.

Don't just look for sex in a marriage – look to make love. Actually look at each other, take the time to see one another, attend to what your spouse wants and needs.

Feeling the heart of your spouse and answering when it calls will give you a new level of sexual intimacy with satisfaction guaranteed.

---

*1 Corinthians 7:5 (NLT)*

*"Do not deprive each other of sexual relations, unless you both agree to refrain from sexual intimacy for a limited time so you can give yourselves more completely to prayer. Afterward, you should come together again so that Satan won't be able to tempt you because of your lack of self-control."*

---

# REFLECTIONS

How many times a week would you like to make love?

........................................................................................................

........................................................................................................

........................................................................................................

What SIMPLE SECRETS give you pleasure from your spouse?

........................................................................................................

........................................................................................................

........................................................................................................

Write down a scripture that speaks to your bedroom love.

........................................................................................................

........................................................................................................

........................................................................................................

........................................................................................................

........................................................................................................

# FORGIVE AND BE FORGIVEN

Apologize when you are wrong, and sometimes even when you aren't. Don't hold grudges, and don't be stubborn. Make up quickly and say you are sorry with a change of heart.

Couples who choose to forgive quickly have a better chance of building each other up and learning how to manage conflict.

---

*Ephesians 4:31-32 (NIV)*

*"Get rid of all bitterness, rage and anger, brawling and slander, along with every form of malice. Be kind and compassionate to one another, forgiving each other, just as in Christ God forgave you."*

---

# REFLECTIONS

In what area has it not been so simple to forgive?

.............................................................................................

.............................................................................................

In what areas do you personally need forgiveness?

.............................................................................................

.............................................................................................

Write a love letter of sincere apology and make a decision to SIMPLY forgive.

.............................................................................................

.............................................................................................

Write down a scripture that speaks to forgiveness.

.............................................................................................

.............................................................................................

.............................................................................................

.............................................................................................

# INVEST IN YOUR MARRIAGE

We invest in furthering our education, getting promoted at work, ministry and church, our children, hobbies, and spending time with friends, but your most important investment should be your spouse.

Do as much as you can, while you can, but never forsake your time of sharing your life with your spouse. Avoid even good distractions that may keep you from relationship-building.

Oftentimes, couples feel unfulfilled in their own marriage, so they begin to fill their lives up with void-fillers, seeking value and affirmation outside of the marriage.

Investing in your marriage should be at the top of the priority list. First the covenant with God, then your spouse, your family, and other commitments.

---

*1 Peter 4:8 (KJV)*

*"And above all things have fervent charity among yourselves: for charity shall cover the multitude of sins."*

---

# REFLECTIONS

In what simple ways can you invest fulfillment in your marriage?

.................................................................................................................

.................................................................................................................

.................................................................................................................

Write down ten ways you will invest in your marriage.

.................................................................................................................

.................................................................................................................

.................................................................................................................

Write down a scripture that speaks to investing in your marriage.

.................................................................................................................

.................................................................................................................

.................................................................................................................

.................................................................................................................

.................................................................................................................

# DATE FOREVER

It is so important to schedule a regular date night for a lifetime. Make this a priority – we can get bitten by the boring bug in our marriage if we don't.

Spice it up and be intentional about scheduling time to romance each other. Sometimes its good to schedule dates with other married friends. It does not replace *your* date night, but it is a bonus to connect with people who have the same values for their marriage.

---

*Proverbs 5:18-19 (ESV)*

*"Let your fountain be blessed, and rejoice in the wife of your youth, a lovely deer, a graceful doe. Let her breast fill you at all times with delight; be intoxicated always in her love."*

---

# REFLECTIONS

Write a list of secret dates for the year, and then repeat annually.

.............................................................................................................

.............................................................................................................

.............................................................................................................

Share your list with your spouse and reflect on how you can achieve your goals.

.............................................................................................................

.............................................................................................................

.............................................................................................................

Write down a scripture that speaks to the beauty of marriage.

.............................................................................................................

.............................................................................................................

.............................................................................................................

.............................................................................................................

.............................................................................................................

# TRY SOMETHING NEW

Switch it up a little! Don't always have the same routine, same meal, same conversation – be spontaneous and change it up a little.

Remember to let your spouse know if the routine is changing; some people don't adjust to change very well. And yes, this will enhance your love.

*Psalm 90:14 (MSG)*

*"Surprise us with love at daybreak; then we'll skip and dance all the day long."*

# REFLECTIONS

Make a SIMPLE list of new things that you are willing to do to get out of your comfort zone.

........................................................................................................

........................................................................................................

........................................................................................................

Write down a scripture that will bring life to your "something new."

........................................................................................................

........................................................................................................

........................................................................................................

Write down a scripture that speaks to new beginnings.

........................................................................................................

........................................................................................................

........................................................................................................

........................................................................................................

# Dream, Dream, & Dream Together

Listen to your spouse's dreams, and share your dreams with your spouse. Some people are not sure of their dreams, and dreams can fade, but never be a dream killer.

Even if does not appear it will ever happen, allow your spouse to have big dreams, and if you are able to help, make their dream come true.

God places dreams in our hearts, so no matter how the enemy comes to try to interrupt your dreams, make sure you both embrace them, pray about them, and by all means, trust God for the outcome. Simply watch them unfold.

---

*Jeremiah 29:11 (ESV)*

*"For I know the plans I have for you, declares the Lord, plans for welfare and not for evil, to give you a future and a hope."*

---

# REFLECTIONS

Write down a list of your personal dreams.

...........................................................................................................................

...........................................................................................................................

...........................................................................................................................

Write down a list of your dreams as a couple.

...........................................................................................................................

...........................................................................................................................

...........................................................................................................................

Write down a scripture that speaks to having dreams and a vision.

...........................................................................................................................

...........................................................................................................................

...........................................................................................................................

...........................................................................................................................

...........................................................................................................................

# Share Responsibilities

Did you know you are on the same team? Don't let something fall apart because it's not your job. We get it twisted sometimes, but as your life grows and your family grows, things change – acknowledge how things have changed, and pitch in where you can to help each other out.

The goal is to share responsibilities; there should never be a tit for tat. Practicing this simple secret can sometimes be hard, but it prevents tension and stress in your marriage.

---

*Ecclesiastes 4:9-10 (MSG)*

*"It's better to have a partner than go it alone. Share the work, share the wealth. And if one falls down, the other helps...."*

---

# REFLECTIONS

List the responsibilities you share together.

......................................................................................................

......................................................................................................

......................................................................................................

List some responsibilities you would like to share together.

......................................................................................................

......................................................................................................

......................................................................................................

Write down a scripture that speaks to working together and sharing life together.

......................................................................................................

......................................................................................................

......................................................................................................

......................................................................................................

......................................................................................................

# TRUST GOD

It's so important to trust God. The biggest mistake couples make is that they begin to solely put their trust in each other.

This does not mean you shouldn't trust your spouse – it literally means recognizing that as married couples and human beings, we will make mistakes in life, but when you solely depend and lean upon God for everything, you can and will live a life full of joy and peace in your marriage.

Life's challenges will present themselves as a point of no return, but if you lean and depend on God, He never fails us. Trust God for your marriage every day.

---

*Proverbs 3:5-6 (NKJV)*

*"Trust in the Lord with all your heart, and lean not on your own understanding; in all your ways acknowledge Him, and He shall direct your paths."*

---

# REFLECTIONS

Do you trust God for your marriage?

..........................................................................................................

..........................................................................................................

..........................................................................................................

Write down a list of testimonies where you have had to trust God.

..........................................................................................................

..........................................................................................................

..........................................................................................................

Write down a scripture that speaks to leaning and depending on God.

..........................................................................................................

..........................................................................................................

..........................................................................................................

..........................................................................................................

..........................................................................................................

# SECRET VISION

Every couple should have a vision for their marriage. What is your vision?

As you thank God for each other, take the time to sit down and write a vision for your marriage. Write down your secrets to love – your formula that reminds you of the reason you got married and fell in love, and what you would like to see in your life together.

Revisit these simple secrets often, and keep working on them to keep the secrets alive!

# REFLECTIONS

Make a list of five or more tips you can offer marriages .

..............................................................................................................

..............................................................................................................

..............................................................................................................

..............................................................................................................

..............................................................................................................

Write down a scripture that encourages us to keep hope alive.

..............................................................................................................

..............................................................................................................

..............................................................................................................

..............................................................................................................

..............................................................................................................

..............................................................................................................

# Wes And Neesha's Top 10 Secret Sayings to Each Other

- You are my best friend.

- I love you.

- You are fine as wine!

- How about a QUICK "E" ?

- The best part of my day is lying here next to you.

- Thank you for loving me.

- I love you.

- Let's pray together.

- Let's stay together forever.

- ????? (too private to print!)

---

*Song of Solomon 6:2 (NLT)*

"My lover has gone down to his garden, to his spice beds,
to browse in the gardens and gather the lilies."

---

# SECRET SPICES FOR INTIMACY

- Thyme – Don't rush, take your THYME

- Allspice – Make it an ALLSPICE night

- Nutmeg – Add some NUTMEG to your apple pie

- Cloves – Make sure your CLOVES are sexy

- Cumin – Both spouses should achieve CUMIN

- Fennel – It's too hot for FENNEL pajamas

- Paprika – A little PAPRIKA might be fun

- Poppy – Love it when you call him Big POPPY

- Red Pepper – Never Crush the RED PEPPER.

- Turmeric – It takes (two) TURMERIC for long-lasting love

- Bonus Option: Excite your spouse with a little pop of Worcestershire BABY. (What this Here) You definitely will get CARAWAY!

# REFLECTIONS

Create a top ten list of your own secret sayings.

.................................................................................................

.................................................................................................

.................................................................................................

Write down scriptures that represent your marriage.

.................................................................................................

.................................................................................................

.................................................................................................

Create your own recipe for intimacy. Be creative, make it fun, and work together!

.................................................................................................

.................................................................................................

.................................................................................................

.................................................................................................

.................................................................................................

# DAILY SECRET POWER

♥ Pray together and put God first for your life, as an individual, and then as a married couple.

♥ Never shut down or shut out your spouse.

♥ Always say "I'm sorry," even if you are not wrong.

♥ Reach out and touch every day – physical touch is vital to a healthy marriage

♥ Invest in your marriage, date regularly, vacation together.

♥ Seek out wise counsel, and never hit a road that's too hard to turn around.

♥ Beware of distractions, even good ones.

♥ Priority is key! You are first in your world! God designed it that way!

www.ingramcontent.com/pod-product-compliance
Lightning Source LLC
LaVergne TN
LVHW051606080426
835510LV00020B/3157